Withdrawn

TEAM EARTH

BENEFICIAL INSECTS
BUGS HELPING PLANTS SURVIVE

BY EMMA HUDDLESTON

CONTENT CONSULTANT
Douglas Golick, PhD
Associate Professor of Entomology
University of Nebraska–Lincoln

Cover image: Ladybugs eat pests including aphids, which can destroy plants.

Core Library

An Imprint of Abdo Publishing
abdobooks.com

abdobooks.com

Published by Abdo Publishing, a division of ABDO, PO Box 398166, Minneapolis, Minnesota 55439. Copyright © 2020 by Abdo Consulting Group, Inc. International copyrights reserved in all countries. No part of this book may be reproduced in any form without written permission from the publisher. Core Library™ is a trademark and logo of Abdo Publishing.

Printed in the United States of America, North Mankato, Minnesota
092019
012020

THIS BOOK CONTAINS RECYCLED MATERIALS

Cover Photo: Henri Koskinen/Shutterstock Images
Interior Photos: Henri Koskinen/Shutterstock Images, 1; Marco Uliana/Shutterstock Images, 4–5 (top); Nigel Cattlin/Science Source, 4–5 (bottom); Shutterstock Images, 8 (ladybug), 8 (mushroom), 8 (plant), 8 (protoist), 8 (bacteria); Paramonov Alexander/Shutterstock Images, 10; iStockphoto, 12–13, 20, 30–31, 33; Annette Shaff/Shutterstock Images, 15, 43; Scott Camazine/ Science Source, 16–17; Leena Robinson/Shutterstock Images, 18; Kent Sievers/Shutterstock Images, 22–23; Jonathan Austin Daniels/iStockphoto, 25, 45; Rijasolo/AFP/Getty Images, 26; Anan Suphap/ Shutterstock Images, 28; Vadym Zaitsev/Shutterstock Images, 34; Tetiana Saienko/Shutterstock Images, 37; Cathy Keifer/iStockphoto, 38–39

Editor: Marie Pearson
Series Designer: Megan Ellis

Library of Congress Control Number: 2019942105

Publisher's Cataloging-in-Publication Data

Names: Huddleston, Emma, author.
Title: Beneficial insects: bugs helping plants survive / by Emma Huddleston
Other title: bugs helping plants survive
Description: Minneapolis, Minnesota : Abdo Publishing, 2020 | Series: Team earth | Includes online resources and index.
Identifiers: ISBN 9781532190971 (lib. bdg.) | ISBN 9781644943243 (pbk.) | ISBN 9781532176821 (ebook)
Subjects: LCSH: Insects as biological pest control agents--Juvenile literature. | Useful insects--Juvenile literature. | Biocontrol agents--Juvenile literature. | Beneficial insects--Juvenile literature. | Insects--Behavior--Juvenile literature.
Classification: DDC 632.9--dc23

CONTENTS

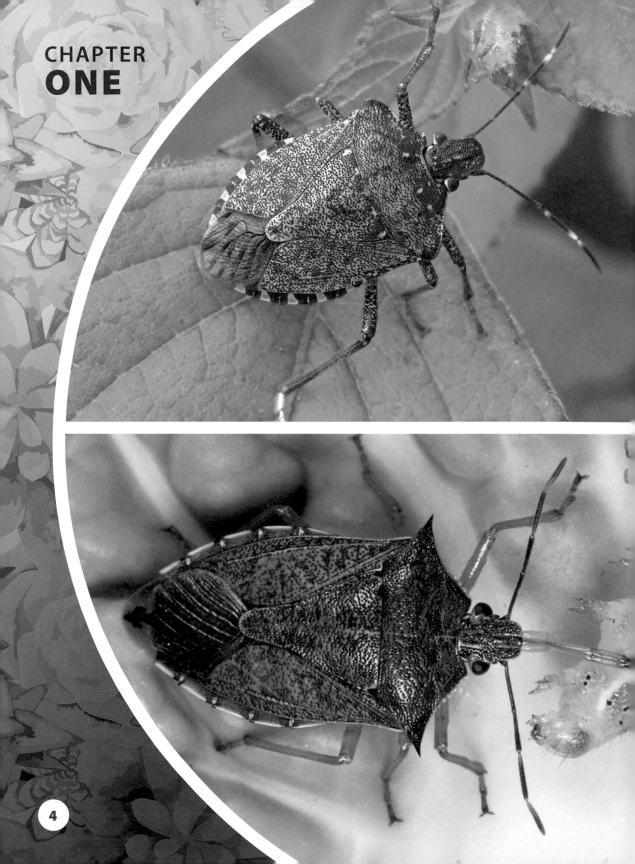

WHAT ARE BENEFICIAL INSECTS?

A spined soldier bug climbs onto a leaf. It has a brown body and pointed shoulders. It is looking for food. The soldier bug looks very similar to a brown marmorated stink bug. Many people get them confused. However, there is an important difference between the two insect species. Brown marmorated stink bugs are invasive in the United States. A living thing is invasive when it enters an environment it did not originate in and then harms the environment. But the soldier bug is a beneficial insect.

One way to tell a brown marmorated stink bug, *top*, from a spined soldier bug, *bottom*, is to look for shoulder spines.

WHAT IS AN INSECT?

All insects share certain features. Insects have exoskeletons and jointed legs. They also have segmented bodies with three major sections. These are the head, thorax, and abdomen. The head has mouthparts, eyes, and a pair of antennae. Antennae are also called feelers. They detect motion and sense smells. Insects use them to gather information about their surroundings. The thorax is the middle section. This is where insects' six legs attach. All insects have three pairs of legs. If the insect has wings, these also attach to the thorax. The abdomen is the rear section. It contains most of the insect's organs.

It protects plants. It eats grasshopper eggs and soft-bodied insects. Instead of being a pest species, it helps get rid of pests.

Pests annoy people. They are the reason people sometimes cringe when thinking of insects. After all, mosquitoes and fleas can carry diseases. Some insects, such as hornets, have a painful sting. Brown marmorated stink bugs smell bad and destroy plants. The problems caused by a few pests can overshadow other species that are beneficial. Beneficial insects help humans and the environment.

INSECTS EVERYWHERE

Insects have been around for 400 million years. They make up approximately 75 percent of all known animal species. Scientists have discovered approximately 1 million insect species. But entomologists, who are scientists who study insects, think there are even more undiscovered insects. They estimate there could be 5 to 10 million living insect species.

Most insects are less than 0.2 inches (6 mm) long. However, insects range in size. The Kirby's walking stick can be 20 inches (50 cm) long. The Hercules moth can have a wingspan up to 10.6 inches (27 cm). The life span of an insect varies greatly from one species to another. Queen termites can live for 50 years. Adult mayflies only live two hours.

Insects have adapted to every land and freshwater habitat. They live in deserts, jungles, glaciers, cold

PERCENTAGES OF
LIVING THINGS

Scientists have described 1.5 million species on Earth. But there are many more species that have yet to be discovered. Most of the known species are insects. But scientists do not think insects make up the largest percentage of living things. Even when combined with all other animals, there are other larger groups. Why might there be more bacteria species in the world, even though scientists know about more insects?

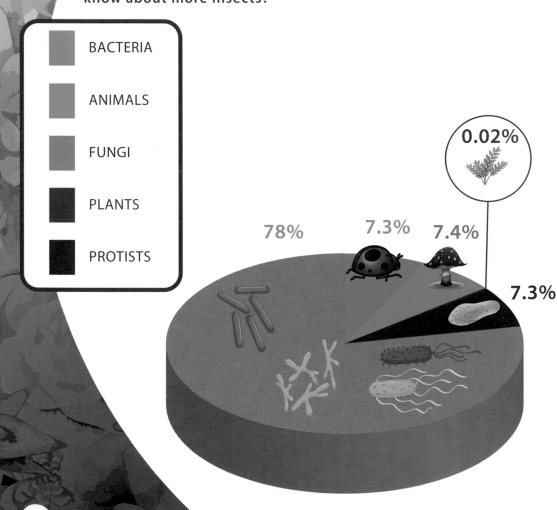

BACTERIA

ANIMALS

FUNGI

PLANTS

PROTISTS

0.02%

78%   7.3%   7.4%   7.3%

streams, and hot springs. They are found around the world. For each person on Earth, scientists estimate there are more than 1 billion insects.

BUGS HELPING PLANTS AND PEOPLE

Most insect species are beneficial to humans and the environment. They help in many ways. Bees pollinate plants. They also make honey, which humans use in medicine and food. Ladybugs prey on plant-eating pests such

THE BEAUTY OF INSECTS

Insects are important for practical and biological reasons, but what about enjoyment? Many people find insects such as colorful beetles and butterflies to be pleasing parts of nature. They are nice to watch fly about and feed on flowering plants. People have enjoyed insects for thousands of years. The Egyptians honored them. They chose a scarab beetle to be a symbol of their sun god. Postage stamps around the world have featured insects. The Jivaro peoples of Ecuador have made earrings with wings of brightly colored beetles.

Many birds eat insects such as mosquitoes.

as aphids. Mosquitoes are food for both bats and birds. Hedgehogs and other small mammals eat insects such as beetles. All insects play a role in the circle of life.

Without beneficial insects, the environment would be unbalanced. Many animals would not have food. Many flowering plants would not be able to reproduce and survive. Fruit, vegetable, and grain crops would get eaten by pests. Beneficial insects may be tiny in size, but they make a big difference in the environment.

STRAIGHT TO THE
SOURCE

David MacNeal's book *Bugged* looks at the roles insects play in the environment. In 2017, MacNeal spoke with *National Geographic* about writing the book:

> *Individually, insects are not incredibly interesting, unless you get down on the ground or view them under a microscope to look at their complexity. But they are the invisible force working throughout the world to keep it running.*
>
> *Almonds in California or watermelons in Florida wouldn't be available if it were not for bees. Insects also return nutrients to the earth. If they weren't around, the amount of decay and rot all over the place would be terrible.*
>
> *We don't notice these services because insects are so small and we often see them as this nuisance. But they are the lever pullers of the world.*

Source: Simon Worrall. "Without Bugs, We Might All Be Dead." *National Geographic*. National Geographic, August 6, 2017. Web. Accessed March 29, 2019.

What's the Big Idea?

Read the text carefully. What is its main idea? Explain how the main idea is supported by two or three details. What does MacNeal mean by calling insects lever pullers?

HEALTHY ENVIRONMENT

Plants cover Earth. They grow in oceans, deserts, jungles, and many other places. Scientists know of 391,000 different plant species, such as flowers and trees, that have tissues that move water and nutrients through the plant. Nutrients, sunlight, and water help plants grow. Together, insects and plants are a part of a global ecosystem that, when healthy, supports many plant and animal species.

Some plants and insects have a mutual relationship. This means they both do work that benefits the other. Some flowering plants produce both nectar and pollen. The blooms,

Pollination is an important way that insects help plants and ecosystems.

scent, and nectar of flowering plants attract insects. Insects use nectar as a food source. In exchange, insects accidentally carry the sticky pollen in the flowers to other flowers. This movement of pollen is called pollination. It helps plants create new seeds to reproduce. More than 87 percent of flowering plants depend on insects for pollination.

PROTECTING EACH OTHER

Another way insects and plants benefit each other is protection. Flowers and plants can

INSECTS SHOW THE ENVIRONMENT'S HEALTH

Insects rely on their environment for nutrients and space to live. So if insects are dying or moving to new areas, scientists monitor them for signs of changes in the environment. A change could be caused by water quality or soil contamination. If the area is healthy, the insects will thrive. Finding more insects than before can also signal a change in the environment. Scientists use insects to study environment quality for a few reasons. Insects live in almost all types of environments. They are easy to handle. Most of all, it is easy to find large numbers of insects.

Bees are well-known pollinators, but other insects, including butterflies, also help pollinate.

provide shelter for insects. At the same time, insects can protect plants from herbivores. Herbivores are insects and other animals that eat plants.

Ants protect acacia trees in Costa Rica. Ants chew back vines that compete with the trees for sunlight. Ants also attack grasshoppers trying to eat the leaves.

Acacia ants protect the acacia trees they live on. In return, they get to eat the nectar the trees make.

In exchange, the trees are food and shelter for the ants. The larvae live in hollow thorns on the branches. The adult ants eat the trees' nectar.

INSECTS' ROLES IN NATURE

Not only do insects help protect plants but they
also support life in other ways. Insects are food for

Green anoles are some of the many reptiles that feed on insects.

other animals. Many fish, birds, and other small animals eat them. Birds around the world eat up to 550 million tons (500 million metric tons) of insects each year. One ton is equal to 2,000 pounds (900 kg). That is approximately the weight of a male bison.

Some insects produce substances that are useful for people. Bees make honey. One type of honey on the Greek island Ikaria is really thick. It has lots of vitamins and nutrients. Local people give credit to the honey for their long life spans. In Ikaria it is common for people to live 90 to 100 years.

Scavengers include beneficial insects that help in decomposition. Decomposition is the process of breaking

PRODUCTS MADE FROM INSECT MATERIALS

Insects provide humans with materials to make products. They create honey, silk, wax, and dyes used in everyday products. Honey is a natural sweetener. The silkworm produces silk. People use silk to make many types of clothing. Aztecs used dye from a scale insect found on prickly pear cacti to color cloth red. Today the insect is still used as dye in food, makeup, and clothing. Beeswax is used in products such as lip balm and hand lotion. Wax from Asian lac insects is used to make shellac, a protective wood coating. Shellac is strong and flexible. It is also used in some nail polishes.

Maggots help dead things break down quickly.

down matter. In nature, this process brings nutrients

back into the soil. For example, when an animal dies,

some insects eat the carcass, or remains. The sun and

wind dry out the body. Then bacteria break down the rest. Insects speed up the process of decomposition. Maggots are the larvae of flies. They eat bacteria on decomposing matter. Blowflies are drawn to fresh carcasses. They lay eggs that develop into maggots. As the decomposition process continues, other insects, such as beetles, also feed on the carcasses. Beetles sometimes eat the maggots too. Other beetles, such as hide beetles, break down keratin found in hair and feathers.

FURTHER EVIDENCE

Chapter Two talks about how some insects pollinate flowers. Identify the main point of the chapter and some key supporting evidence. Then look at the website below. Find a quote that supports the chapter's main point. Does the quote support a piece of evidence already in the chapter? Or does it add a new piece of information?

THE LIFE CYCLE OF FLOWERING PLANTS
abdocorelibrary.com/beneficial-insects

PEST CONTROL

While some insect species are harmful, only 3 percent of the nearly 1 million known insect species are pests. Some pest insects attack crops and livestock. Others carry disease. Harmful insect species put human food sources and lives in danger. This is why humans sometimes use tools to control the numbers of harmful insects.

Insect pests can cause two types of damage to plants and animals. Indirect damage happens when the insect itself doesn't cause harm. Instead, by feeding on a plant or animal, it passes on a disease. Mosquitoes often cause indirect damage to humans.

Some insect pests, such as the Japanese beetle in the United States, can damage or kill plants.

USING INSECTS FOR SCIENCE

Some pest species are used in research. Their unique bodies could lead to better medicine. Cockroaches are known as pests because they are difficult to kill. They also live in some of the dirtiest parts of our cities and towns. Yet somehow they stay clean and healthy. Scientists are looking to them for cures. Fruit flies are used often in genetic research. This is partially because they reproduce quickly. This quality can be annoying to humans when the flies swarm a fruit tree. But it is helpful in research. Studying disease in fruit flies helps scientists understand how humans resist diseases and infection. Also, due to their quick growth, scientists can quickly see how genes are passed from one generation to another.

Mosquitoes feed on blood. Some species pass on diseases such as malaria to humans when feeding. Another type of damage is direct damage. This happens to plants when insects eat or burrow into plant stems, fruit, or roots. Hundreds of insect species cause direct damage. This is the more common type of damage.

Aphids are plant pests. They are tiny insects with soft bodies. They cause

Aphids are pests. Ladybugs eat aphids, which keeps aphid populations under control.

direct damage to plants by sucking the sugary juices from plants. Aphids can seriously harm plants. Aphids can keep a plant from reaching its full size, pass on diseases, and cause abnormal plant growths and deformed leaves, buds, and flowers.

BLAMING INSTINCT

Humans have instincts. Instincts are actions done in response to something in the environment. An example of an instinct is running from something that

Swarms of locusts can quickly devour crops.

is frightening. This is a response that aims to keep someone safe. However, humans' brains are more advanced than those of insects. People have control over their thoughts and actions. A person might feel the urge to run away but can decide to not move. Insects do not have control of their actions. They behave based on instinct. Some actions they do are harmless in their natural environments but cause problems for humans.

Many insects eat organic matter, including crops and wood. This feeding can be harmful for people. Some insects eat crops growing in the field. Others eat the products, such as fruits, vegetables, or grains, while they are being stored.

Insects such as termites are beneficial when they break down dead trees in the wild. But they are harmful when they eat and break down wood used in buildings. Termite damage can weaken buildings, making the structures dangerous to humans. Other insects such as clothes moths and carpet beetles chew holes into clothes and carpets.

INSECT PREDATORS

Beneficial insects help control the populations of pests. Insect predators are one type of beneficial insect. Predators eat animals. These predators can help create balance in

BENEFICIAL PARASITES

Some wasps are parasites. Parasites live or feed on another living creature, called a host. Sometimes the host dies so the parasite species can live on. Some parasitic wasps lay their eggs inside pest species such as caterpillars. The eggs develop and grow. Young wasps hatch from the eggs. These larval wasps feed on the caterpillars. The feeding eventually kills the caterpillars. Some caterpillars eat holes in leaves and cause plants to die. Wasps are their natural predator and natural pest control.

Dragonflies are one of many insects that help control insect populations.

the environment. Predators keep the numbers of other species from growing too large. Ladybugs eat aphids. Ground beetles eat insects that live on the ground. Dragonflies eat insects that fly. Praying mantises eat anything they can find. These insects are natural pest control in the wild.

A diverse number of different insects is a sign of a healthy environment. This is even true for a small home garden. A healthy garden has enough sunlight, water, and space for plants to grow. It has a variety of plants. These features attract a variety of insects. Many insects that live in gardens are beneficial. They eat the pests. They also rely on flowering plants. Many beneficial insects get nutrients from pollen and nectar too. They also need water. Having a small pond, stream, or puddle makes it easy for them to get water. However, unhealthy garden plants that are diseased or wilting are more attractive to pests. It is easier for pests to damage sick plants. That is why it's important to take care of plants.

EXPLORE ONLINE

Chapter Three discusses pests. The article below goes into more depth on one type of pest. As you know, every source is different. How is the information from the website the same as the information in Chapter Three? What new information have you learned?

NATIONAL WILDLIFE FEDERATION: INVASIVE SPECIES

abdocorelibrary.com/beneficial-insects

LIVING WITH INSECTS

While most insects are beneficial, many people work to reduce insect populations by killing them. They try to get rid of some insects, especially pests. Chemical pest control is a common method for dealing with insects. If misused, these chemicals can be harmful to both humans and animals.

Dangerous chemicals get into water and food. People accidentally eat them. Farmers and people who work or live near farms with pesticides are at extra risk. Chemicals can get on their clothes or skin. According to the

Some people treat their gardens and homes with pesticides.

World Health Organization (WHO), education is one way to decrease the negative impacts of pesticides. The WHO also encourages farmers to use other methods of pest control instead of only relying on pesticides.

But a complete ban on chemicals isn't the solution either. Some chemicals, when used correctly, save lives. For example, some kill mosquitoes that carry deadly malaria.

PESTICIDE PROBLEMS

Scientists in the United Kingdom studied the decline in insect populations. They found habitat danger was a major threat to insects. Pesticides protect crops from insects. But the chemicals can also harm plants, other animals, and people. This can happen when the chemical pesticides are misused. For example, if some pesticides are applied to blooming plants, bees visiting the flowers to collect pollen and nectar can be harmed or killed by these pesticides.

SAFE SOLUTIONS

Humans need to learn how to live with insects. An insect extinction would be devastating for all levels of life. The worlds of plants,

Cherry farmers can use yellow sticky traps to monitor western cherry fruit flies.

animals, and humans are all connected to insects. One solution to pest control is integrated pest management (IPM). IPM can help control insects in large areas, such as farms. It has four steps. It requires farmers to be aware of different types of insects.

First, farmers monitor their crops to see what pests they have. One method is to use traps. The number collected in traps shows how serious their pest situation is. If pest populations are low, there might be little risk to the crops. If populations are higher, their crops could be at risk. Second, farmers make physical changes to

improve the situation. It is best to use several methods. Farmers might add netting around vegetable plants. They might also use beneficial insects as a natural pest control.

Third, farmers might also need to use chemical control. The IPM approach supports using pesticides only as a last option. Pesticides are only used after knowing if there is a likelihood of bad crop loss and after trying all other strategies. Additionally, pesticides are only recommended if they do not harm beneficial insects. Farmers are careful to use the pesticide in a way that is least risky for beneficial insects. Finally, farmers check to see if the pests are now under control. If not, farmers will adjust the methods they are using.

MOVING FORWARD

A positive relationship between humans and insects includes sharing the same environment. Humans often work to protect insects. The public, scientists,

Netting can protect crops from pests.

LAWS ABOUT PESTICIDES

The Environmental Protection Agency (EPA) makes rules to protect the environment. Some people think the EPA is not strict enough. In 2019, the allowed pesticides weren't protecting cotton and sorghum crops from pests. Bees are attracted to those plants. They eat the nectar. The EPA allowed farmers to use sulfoxaflor on the crops in 18 US states. The pesticide is not usually allowed. It harms bees. Some people think the EPA should ban this pesticide. Others note that there are ways to use the pesticide that reduce damage to bees. Regardless of the rules, individuals can always make decisions to use fewer products that could hurt bees.

conservation organizations, and the US government built a butterfly highway. It follows Interstate 35, a large highway that runs from Minnesota to the US–Mexico border. Milkweed was planted in open spaces along and around the roadway. This milkweed is food for monarch caterpillars. It is the only plant that monarch butterfly larvae can eat. Monarch butterflies migrate from Canada to Mexico each year.

INSECTS AS
PEST CONTROL

A main way beneficial insects help humans is as natural pest control. How does the information in the chart compare to what you read in the text? How could one of these bugs change the environment where you live?

BENEFICIAL INSECT	PLANTS THAT ATTRACT IT	PESTS IT EATS
GROUND BEETLE	• AMARANTH • BUNCH GRASSES	• SLUGS • SNAILS • GYPSY MOTHS • CATERPILLARS
LACEWING	• CARROTS • SUNFLOWERS • GOLDENRODS	• APHIDS • MEALYBUGS • SCALES • MITES
LADYBUG	• BUTTERFLY WEED • NATIVE GRASSES • GIANT HYSSOP • YARROW	• APHIDS • SPIDER MITES • MEALYBUGS
SPIDER	• CARROTS • DAISIES • SUNFLOWERS • YARROW • GOLDENRODS • GIANT HYSSOP	• MANY INSECT PESTS

Monarch butterfly caterpillars rely on milkweed for food.

Along their migration, the milkweed provides a place to lay their eggs.

Another way people learn to appreciate the value of insects is by eating them. Approximately 80 percent of people on Earth eat insects. Insects as food are an important part of some people's cultural heritage.

Grasshoppers mixed with
spices are sold in Mexico. They can add
nutrients to a meal. Caterpillars are popular in many
African countries, including Zimbabwe. They are also
a great source of calcium and iron. It is important to
remember that removing too many insects from the

environment for food can be harmful to the balance of nature. It is better to eat farm-raised, sustainable insects. Something is sustainable if it can be used again and again without running out. Eating insects can be more sustainable than eating other sources of meat. It doesn't take much food or water to raise them. They also take up less space. Other meat sources, such as cows and pigs, take more space and resources to raise per pound of protein that they produce.

Beneficial insects are an important part of the world. They protect plants that keep the environment healthy. They help crops grow. They provide food for animals and people. Pest predators help balance the number of insects in nature. By learning about the value of insects to humans, people will better protect them. The next step is learning how to live with them.

STRAIGHT TO THE
SOURCE

Entomologists John Losey and Mace Vaughan calculated how much money insects add to the US economy. Susan S. Lang explained their findings in an article:

> *The study found that native insects are food for the wildlife supporting a $50 billion recreation industry and provide more than $4.5 billion worth in pest control. They also provide crop pollination valued at $3 billion and clean up grazing lands, saving ranchers some $380 million a year.*
>
> *Insects are an integral part of a complex web of interactions that helps put food on our tables and remove our wastes. Humans—and probably most life on Earth—would perish without insects, Vaughan said.*

> Source: Susan S. Lang. "Careful with That Bug!" *Cornell Chronicle*. Cornell University, April 1, 2006. Web. Accessed March 29, 2019.

Back It Up

The author of this passage is using evidence to support a point. Write a paragraph describing the point the author is making. Then write down two or three pieces of evidence the author uses to make the point.

FAST FACTS

- Scientists have discovered more than 1 million insect species. They estimate there could be 5 to 10 million total insect species.

- Beneficial insects help plants and people. They provide food for other species, pollinate plants, produce useful substances, act as pest control, and decompose dead matter.

- Plants and insects have a mutual relationship. They help each other survive and create healthy environments.

- Insects behave based on instinct. Sometimes this results in problems for humans.

- Pest species can harm crops and spread disease. They can be controlled by chemical pesticides, through crop rotation, and through natural insect predators.

- Integrated pest management is a step-by-step method for managing pests. It aims to help farmers identify if there is a problem, inform management approaches, and effectively and safely control pests.

STOP AND THINK

Say What?
Studying insects and the environment can mean learning a lot of new vocabulary. Find five words in this book you've never heard before. Use a dictionary to find out what they mean. Then write the meanings in your own words, and use each word in a new sentence.

Surprise Me
Chapter Two discusses different kinds of beneficial insects. After reading this book, what two or three facts about insects did you find most surprising? Write a few sentences about each fact. Why did you find each fact surprising?

Why Do I Care?
Maybe you do not live on a farm or have a garden. But your life would still be a lot different without beneficial insects. How would the foods you eat be different if insects did not pollinate crops? What would nature be like without insects to break down waste?

Another View

Chapter Three discusses pest problems. As you know, every source is different. Ask a librarian or another adult to help you find another source about pests. Write a short essay comparing and contrasting the new source's point of view with that of this book's author. What is the point of view of each author? How are they similar and why? How are they different and why?

GLOSSARY

ecosystem
a community of living things and their surroundings and how they work together

exoskeleton
a shell-like skin and supportive structure on the outside of the body

gene
something passed on from parents to offspring that influences different traits

keratin
a protein found in hair and nails

larva
an early form of an insect that hatches from an egg; usually wormlike

migrate
to routinely travel from one area to another

nectar
a sweet and sticky substance produced by plants

organic
a product made from substances that were once living

pesticide
a chemical substance created by humans to kill pest species

pollinate
to transfer pollen from the male part of a flower to the female part of a flower

species
a group of animals that share similar features, lifestyles, and abilities and are able to breed together

ONLINE
RESOURCES

To learn more about beneficial insects, visit our free resource websites below.

Visit **abdocorelibrary.com** or scan this QR code for free Common Core resources for teachers and students, including vetted activities, multimedia, and booklinks, for deeper subject comprehension.

Visit **abdobooklinks.com** or scan this QR code for free additional online weblinks for further learning. These links are routinely monitored and updated to provide the most current information available.

LEARN
MORE

Hamilton, S. L. *Bees & Wasps*. Minneapolis, MN: Abdo Publishing, 2015.

McCarthy, Cecilia Pinto. *Monarch Butterflies Matter*. Minneapolis, MN: Abdo Publishing, 2016.

INDEX

About the Author

Emma Huddleston lives in the Twin Cities with her husband. She enjoys writing educational books, but she likes reading novels even more. When she is not writing or reading, she likes to stay active by running and swing dancing.